Voices of Leadership

Voices of Leadership

POEMS INSPIRED BY US PRESIDENT

Joel Hawksley

J & Washington Network

Contents

INTRODUCTION

From the foundational whispers of Washington to the re-sounding declarations of modern leaders, this collection breathes new life into the words of America's presidents.

For centuries, the voices of our nation's leaders have guided, inspired, and shaped the course of history. Their quotes, like beacons of light, offer wisdom and insight that transcend their time. Yet, sometimes, these historical gems can feel distant and untouchable.

This book endeavors to capture the vibrancy and warmth of these timeless quotes by transforming them into the expressive language of poetry. Each poem acts as a brushstroke, delicately illuminating the essence of the original quote. It's not about replacing their words, but rather about revealing their hidden depths and emotions.

Imagine Abraham Lincoln's powerful reflections transformed into poignant verses of unity, or John F. Kennedy's stirring call to purpose blossoming into a narrative of inspiration. This book invites you to experience these quotes anew, not just with your intellect, but with your heart.

While I may not claim the title of a poet, I hope these humble creations spark a connection with the wisdom and strength embedded within our presidential legacy. Whether you're a seasoned reader of poetry or someone who appreciates the power of words, I invite you to delve into this collection and let the verses sing their own unique song.

From the quiet resolve found in early leadership to the bold visions of the modern era, these poems celebrate the resilience, courage, and determination that define the American spirit. May they inspire you to embrace your own path with renewed determination and hope.

1

George Washington

"Associate yourself with men of good quality if you esteem your own reputation; for 'tis better to be alone than in bad company."

In solitude's embrace,
Better to stand alone,
Than in falsehood's chase,
Find your reputation's throne.

2

John Adams

"To be good, and to do good, is all we have to do."

In the quiet act of doing good,
Life's purpose is found.
In the simplest of deeds,
Humanity's greatness is crowned.

3

Thomas Jefferson

"Nothing can stop the man with the right mental attitude from achieving his goal; nothing on earth can help the man with the wrong mental attitude."

With a mind set on the stars,
No obstacle too great.
But a heart weighed down,
Will never find its fate.

4

James Madison

"The circulation of confidence is better than the circulation of money."

Confidence, like gold,
Shall in hearts reside.
Wealth in spirit bold,
No currency can hide.

5

James Monroe

"It is by a thorough knowledge of the whole subject that [people] are enabled to judge correctly of the past and to give a proper direction to the future."

In knowledge vast,
Our future finds its way.
Through wisdom of the past,
We guide tomorrow's day.

6

John Quincy Adams

"If your actions inspire others to dream more, learn more, do more and become more, you are a leader."

In dreams you spark,
And actions clear,
A leader's mark,
In hearts sincere.

7

Andrew Jackson

"Any man worth his salt will stick up for what he believes right, but it takes a slightly better man to acknowledge instantly and without reservation that he is in error."

In strength we hold,
What we deem as right.
Yet stronger, bold,
To admit in wrong, our sight.

$$\boxed{8}$$

Martin Van Buren

"It is easier to do a job right than to explain why you didn't."

In effort true,
No need to explain.
For work done through,
Leaves no room for pain.

William Henry Harrison

"Times change, and we change with them."

As seasons shift,
So must we grow.
In time's swift drift,
Our path we sow.

John Tyler

"I can never consent to being dictated to."

In freedom's light,
My spirit's call,
To stand in right,
And never fall.

11

James K. Polk

"The gratitude ... should be commensurate with the boundless blessings which we enjoy."

In gratitude,
Our hearts shall sing.
For blessings wide,
In life, we cling.

12

Zachary Taylor

"I have always done my duty. I am ready to die. My only regret is for the friends I leave behind me."

Duty's call,
I answered well.
In life's final fall,
In friendships, dwell.

13

Millard Fillmore

"An honorable defeat is better than a dishonorable victory."

In defeat, honor's glow,
In victory, false might.
Better to stand low,
Than high in dishonor's light.

14

Franklin Pierce

"While men inhabiting different parts of this vast continent cannot be expected to hold the same opinions, they can unite in a common objective and sustain common principles."

In unity's bind,
Diverse as we are.
Common goals we'll find,
Together, reach far.

15

James Buchanan

"The test of leadership is not to put greatness into humanity, but to elicit it, for the greatness is already there."

In each soul's light,
Greatness does reside.
A leader's gentle might,
Brings it to the tide.

Abraham Lincoln

"I don't like that man. I must get to know him better."

In dislike's grasp,
Empathy will grow.
In understanding's clasp,
True connections flow.

17

Andrew Johnson

"If you always support the correct principles then you will never get the wrong results!"

In principles,
Our guide does rest.
In their pursuit,
We find our best.

$$\boxed{18}$$

Gen. Ulysses S. Grant

"In every battle there comes a time when both sides consider themselves beaten, then he who continues the attack wins."

In battle's strife,
When hope seems thin.
Persist in life,
And you shall win.

Rutherford B. Hayes

"Every expert was once a beginner."

From humble start,
Great skills are honed.
In every heart,
A master is known.

20

James A. Garfield

"Right reason is stronger than force."

In reason's hand,
True strength is found.
Force may demand,
But wisdom is crowned.

21

Chester A. Arthur

"Be fit for more than the thing you are now doing. Let everyone know that you have a reserve in yourself; that you have more power than you are now using. If you are not too large for the place you occupy, you are too small for it."

In potential vast,
Our strength does lie.
More than the present,
Our limits defy.

22

Grover Cleveland

"It is better to be defeated standing for a high principle than to run by committing subterfuge."

In principle's light,
Stand tall, though defeat.
In subterfuge slight,
No honor's seat.

23

Benjamin Harrison

"Great lives never go out; they go on."

In legacy,
Lives continue.
In memory,
We renew.

William McKinley

"In the time of darkest defeat, victory may be nearest."

In darkness deep,
Hope's light does gleam.
In defeat, we keep,
Victory's dream.

25

Theodore Roosevelt

"If you could kick the person in the pants responsible for most of your trouble, you wouldn't sit for a month."

In jest we find,
Our troubles' cause.
With humor kind,
We pause.

William Howard Taft

"We must dare to be great; and we must realize that greatness is the fruit of toil and sacrifice and high courage."

In daring, great,
In toil's embrace.
In courage's fate,
We find our place.

27

Woodrow Wilson

"The object of love is to serve, not to win."

In love's true aim,
Service does lie.
Not in victory's name,
But in giving, we fly.

28

Warren G. Harding

"There's good in everybody. Boost. Don't knock."

In every soul,
Goodness does shine.
In support, our goal,
In kindness, divine.

29

Calvin Coolidge

"If you see ten troubles coming down the road, you can be sure that nine will run into the ditch before they reach you."

In troubles' sight,
Patience is key.
Most will alight,
And leave us be.

30

Herbert Hoover

"Be patient and calm; no one can catch a fish with anger."

In calm, we find,
Life's gentle flow.
In patience kind,
Success will grow.

31

Franklin D. Roosevelt

"Men are not prisoners of fate, but only prisoners of their own minds."

In mind's domain,
Our freedom's kept.
In thought's refrain,
Our fate is leapt.

32

Harry S. Truman

"It is amazing what you can accomplish if you do not care who gets the credit."

In selfless acts,
Greatness is sown.
In shared pacts,
Achievements are known.

33

Dwight D. Eisenhower

"Pessimism never won any battle."

In optimism bright,
Victory does bloom.
In hope's light,
We dispel gloom.

John F. Kennedy

"Efforts and courage are not enough without purpose and direction."

In effort grand,
And courage strong.
Purpose's hand,
Guides us along.

Lyndon B. Johnson

"Yesterday is not ours to recover, but tomorrow is ours to win or lose."

In tomorrow's dawn,
Our fate does lie.
Yesterday gone,
In future, we try.

Richard M. Nixon

"Remember, always give your best. Never get discouraged. Never be petty. Always remember, others may hate you. But those who hate you don't win unless you hate them. And then you destroy yourself."

In best we give,
In discouragement's fall.
In love, we live,
In hate, we stall.

37

Gerald R. Ford

"Never be satisfied with less than your very best effort. If you strive for the top and miss, you'll still 'beat the pack.'"

In striving high,
Though we may miss.
In effort's try,
We find our bliss.

Jimmy Carter

"You can do what you have to do, and sometimes you can do it even better than you think you can."

In need's call,
Our strength is found.
In effort tall,
Exceeding bounds.

39

Ronald Reagan

"Heroes may not be braver than anyone else. They're just braver five minutes longer."

In courage's face,
A hero stands.
In lasting grace,
Bravery commands.

40

George H. W. Bush

"No problem of human making is too great to be overcome by human ingenuity, human energy, and the untiring hope of the human spirit."

In spirit's might,
No problem grand.
In hope's light,
We firmly stand.

41

Bill Clinton

"If you live long enough, you'll make mistakes. But if you learn from them, you'll be a better person. It's how you handle adversity, not how it affects you. The main thing is never quit, never quit, never quit."

In mistakes, we find,
Life's learning path.
In adversity, kind,
Our strength's aftermath.

42

George W. Bush

"A leadership is someone who brings people together."

In unity's call,
Leadership's grace.
Together, stand tall,
In shared space.

43

Barack Obama

"Change will not come if we wait for some other person or some other time. We are the ones we've been waiting for. We are the change that we seek."

In our hands,
Change does reside.
In action's bands,
We turn the tide.

44

Donald Trump

"Without passion you don't have energy, without energy you have nothing."

In passion's fire,
Energy's blaze.
In life's desire,
Achievement's phase.

45

Joe Biden

"Fighting corruption is not just good governance. It's self-defense. It's patriotism."

In governance fair,
Corruption's fight.
In patriotism's care,
We guard our right.

About the Author

Joel Hawksley has always been drawn to the power of words. Born into a world of contradictions and complexities, he found solace and expression in poetry from an early age. His journey as a poet began as a way to navigate and make sense of the world around him—a world filled with both beauty and profound historical significance.

Growing up, Joel was fascinated by the works of literary greats and the profound impact of historical figures. He saw how history could reveal deeper truths, often hidden beneath layers of time and interpretation. This fascination led him to hone his craft, developing a voice that is both reflective and insightful.

Joel's career has been as varied as the themes he explores in his poetry. From politics and business to his time in the US Army, he has experienced the many facets of human endeavor and history. These experiences have provided a rich tapestry of material for his poetic work, allowing him to write with authenticity and depth.

For 37 years, poetry was a private form of journaling, a way to cope with life's challenges and celebrate its moments of significance. It is only recently that Joel began to share his work with the world, hoping to bring reflection, understanding, and perhaps a bit of inspiration to those who read his words.

This historical poetry collection is a culmination of Joel Hawksley's journey as a poet. It is a testament to his belief in the power of historical wisdom to illuminate our present and future, and to his unwavering commitment to exploring the narratives that have shaped our society.

As Joel continues to write, he remains dedicated to using poetry as a tool for historical reflection, ever hopeful that his words will inspire others to see the world with a deeper appreciation for the past and a thoughtful eye toward the future.

www.ingramcontent.com/pod-product-compliance
Lightning Source LLC
Chambersburg PA
CBHW052337150726
47998CB00018B/2386